Corporate America's Misbehaving Children

By

Marjorie Wooster & Sandra Simoneaux

authorHOUSE

1663 LIBERTY DRIVE, SUITE 200
BLOOMINGTON, INDIANA 47403
(800) 839-8640
WWW.AUTHORHOUSE.COM

This book is a work of fiction. Places, events, and situations in this story are purely fictional and any resemblance to actual persons, living or dead, is coincidental.

© 2004 Marjorie Wooster & Sandra Simoneaux.
All Rights Reserved.

No part of this book may be reproduced, stored in a retrieval system, or transmitted by any means without the written permission of the author.

First published by AuthorHouse 10/25/04

ISBN: 1-4184-9423-2 (e)
ISBN: 1-4184-9422-4 (sc)

Library of Congress Control Number: 2004096450

Printed in the United States of America
Bloomington, Indiana

This book is printed on acid-free paper.

Table of Contents

Chapter 1 Only Three Months Old – Everything Is A WONDER 1

Chapter 2 Six Months Old, Yelling & Screaming When Annoyed .. 4

Chapter 3 Twelve Months And Showing Apprehension Around Strangers 6

Chapter 4 I'm Two And Can Play Make-Believe! 8

Chapter 5 Yes I'm Three 10

Chapter 6 What Is Real And What Is Imaginary At Four 14

Chapter 7 Inventing Games And Rules 17

Chapter 8 Six And Venturing Out 19

Chapter 9 Developing an Awareness of Time and Money at Seven 22

Chapter 10 At Eight, We Love To Share Stories..................... 25

Chapter 11 The Nine-Year Old Bully 27

Chapter 12 Ten And Challenging Parental Authority & Society Rules 30

Chapter 13 The Need To Know And Understand Everything At Eleven! 34

Chapter 14 How Do I look?... 36

Chapter 15 Pushing The Bar As A New Teenager................... 38

Chapter 16 The World Revolves Around Only Me 43

Chapter 17 Sixteen & Seventeen – SEX! SEX! SEX! SEX! SEX! SEX! SEX! 45

Chapter 18 Eighteen And In Charge Of My Own Destiny 49

Chapter 19 It All Happened So Fast! 53

Chapter 20 The Body Count 57

v

Foreword

This book is dedicated first to our husbands, Jeff and Joey, for all the times they were there to add words of encouragement and humor or just sit and listen to us unload when we came home totally drained from babysitting all of "our children" and secondly to all Human Resources professionals who must deal with the childish and adolescent behaviors of the employees, managers, and top executives of Corporate America on a daily basis and continually struggle with themselves to maintain the dignity and professionalism required of their positions. As many Human Resource professionals will attest to, being a "parent" in a large dysfunctional family is extremely challenging but can also be very rewarding when we see responsible adult behavior displayed, even if infrequently.

We never could have written this book without experiencing firsthand the extraordinary experience of raising children. We are constantly amazed at the similarities between employee behavior at all levels in an organization to the different stages we encountered and fortunately survived and continue to endure and survive in our own children's maturation stages from infants to adulthood. Our children, Pat, Gene, Tracie, Laura, Michael, Jeremy, Justin and Aimee prepared us for all of the challenges we would face in our careers in human resources. Aimee, Justin, Laura, Jeremy, and Michael still provide us with valuable analogies as they continue to strive to reach adulthood. Between all of our children, we continue to experience all phases from infancy to adulthood that has prepared us to cope with the adult child in Corporate America. Our children's contribution to this book is immeasurable and greatly appreciated.

Introduction

There are many stages that children go through from birth to adulthood. Some of the stages are a joy for parents to be a part of, such as when the toddler first begins to walk and explore things that were out of their reach before. Then there are some childhood stages especially in the adolescent years that can challenge a parent's love and patience to the maximum limit. Most children move through each stage successfully and mature emotionally and mentally into responsible, compassionate, caring adults. Sometimes though, a child just never seems to conquer a particular stage in their development and continues to move into the next stage with an unresolved maturation step. They reach adulthood still possessing the behavior trait that was never dealt with successfully in their childhood years. This stage of arrested development affects everyone they interact with through out their life if not recognized and resolved.

Most of us do carry some piece of our childhood with us as we grow and develop and move into the adult world. Generally these childish traits that we hang on to are harmless and can even enrich our lives, such as harmless pranks, games and innocent play. It is the childish behavior that is harmful and destructive to themselves and others and was never resolved and coped with at the proper stage in the person's maturation process that this book discusses. With thirty plus years working with employees at all levels in Corporate America, we have dealt with most of these unresolved maturation stages in "adults". They are not pretty to witness and can be very difficult to deal with.

It is imperative for the reader to note that the characters presented in this publication are fictional and for entertainment purposes only. The authors and publisher make no claim as to the accuracy of the information and will not accept any liability for any loss or damage, which may be incurred by any person acting in reliance upon the information. This publication is protected by copyright. No part may be reproduced by any process except in accordance with the provisions of the Copyright Act of 1968.

Corporate America's Misbehaving Children

Chapter 1
Only Three Months Old - Everything Is A WONDER

There you are, in a new job and feeling proud, exhilarated by the new opportunity yet also feeling small, clueless, afraid and glancing around with wonder. The people seem friendly enough; yet curious, and you're not real sure if you remember the hallway to get to your cubicle. This new surrounding is mysterious. Does this remind you of a small child? Say, birth to three months old perhaps?

For those of us that have children, this age is wonderful to observe as a parent. Your little one is amazed and looks around at the wonder of it all. The trees, open spaces, the mobile in the crib, animals and all of the loving words from happy big faces. This is a stage of complete fascination with the world and its unknown aspects. Everyone seems to be so delighted to meet you. Does it also sound like your new job? It's a time of expectation yet fear.

So, you sit in your new office or cubicle after hours of orientation and begin putting all these new things together in your mind. The new kid on the block has to learn quickly for management is watching. You take everything in like an infant. You scan your environment, try to remember names, departments, and let's not forget the company mission statement.

The hours turn into days, the days into months, the months into years and this sense of wonder is slowly replaced by a sense of caution. Suddenly, the new opportunity doesn't seem so friendly; everyone isn't as nice as they seemed at first. One slowly comes to realize that it's a job and it's hard work! Who can you trust? Who will catch you if you fall? As an infant, you must trust that someone is looking out for your best interest. Well, unfortunately in the working world, your co-workers and dare say "Your Boss" are not so concerned with your basic needs of food, clothing, shelter or survival. It's work and who ever said it has to be fun is the new mission statement you've adopted as the years have progressed.

As we say in Human Resources, the Honeymoon Phase is over now and we just try and "stay together for the children". Change can be very disruptive and disruption affects the bottom line.

In this early stage of development, the infant also quickly begins to learn how to control their environment and everyone in it. The infant cries and the parents and siblings jump to attention, scrambling to figure out what they need to do to meet the infant's prevailing need and stop the incessant crying. They will do anything and the infant, after a very short time, revels in the power he or she holds over everyone. The infant's circle of influence extends to anyone who comes into his or her environment.

Unfortunately, for some this need for total control and inner focus is never replaced with the "team" concept towards others. They continue to go through life expecting everything and everyone in their environment to be at their mercy.

Minnie Perfect was the "Ralph Kranden" of the business world and was one of those "micro" managers and to top it off, she was also an alcoholic. This combination was deadly to those she supervised and her peers. She could have co-workers and her staff in tears over her constant criticism of how they performed their work. Never mind that Minnie had a strong voice that carried her cutting and critical tirades across every cubicle in the victim's department area. This was of no concern to Minnie. She was only focused on making sure that everyone in her department did everything the way she wanted, right down to the last detail. If

Minnie was challenged by one of her staff or another manager, she would berate their idea or method very loudly, stomp around the office growling at everyone who crossed her path, becoming very confrontational, slamming items down on her desk in disgust, all along mumbling under her breath making everyone within earshot very uncomfortable and looking for a quick escape route. Everyone knew that Minnie would not hesitate a second to throw others in front of the bus if they dared to criticize her or make her department look bad. Her infantile behavior would continue and escalate until all opposition collapsed and everyone capitulated to her way. Peace would once again be restored in the office when Minnie was happy and back in control.

Chapter 2
Six Months Old, Yelling & Screaming When Annoyed

Infants grow at a tremendous rate during their first year of growth and by six months of age they are communicating pain, fear, loneliness, discomfort or disapproval by crying with tears. On an intellectual level, the six-month old is exploring objects, putting everything in his or her mouth, playing with fingers, toes, hands and responds to sounds and color with such awe. This is also the time to develop a sense of trust and security. The feeling of security encourages the desire to learn new things. The feeling of insecurity reaps crying; yelling and screaming when annoyed.

The emotions and behavior of a six-month-old often surface in the office. Samantha Clinger, a CPA by profession spent long hours in her small corner office crunching numbers to her boss's satisfaction. She often stayed hunched over her desk in complete wonder of all the numbers, signs and symbols that represented success in her mind. Much like the six-month-old who admires her toes for the first time in the crib, Samantha was awed at how she could push and crunch, push and crunch the numbers to absolute perfection and obtain the approval of her manager, Amanda Power. Each time Amanda praised Samantha for a job well done, she beamed with a smile and sense of security. She would ask for more assignments, the opportunity to learn new things and receive more approval from her manager.

One Monday morning, Samantha proudly presented her latest project result to Amanda after working all weekend. Samantha just couldn't wait for a response; she hung on every anticipated word from Amanda's mouth. Unfortunately, on this day, Amanda was not so pleased with Samantha's work and noted that she could not accept this project. There was an unspoken sense of darkness and annoyance in the room. Samantha questioned her methods and pleaded with Amanda to tell her what she had done wrong. Amanda just sat and glared at Samantha with a stern face of disapproval. Samantha's world was crumbling. The colors of her world were turning from red to blue. A disappointed Samantha took her project back to her desk and sat in dismay. Moments later, she began to cry. She had to fight back her primal urge to yell and scream! The bottom line had become blurry. Samantha needed someone to comfort and reassure her, to bring back the secure feeling that was desperately needed. She needed her Mommy.

Susie Anxious was never able to move out of the uncertain phase of the six month old. She appeared to be stuck in the insecure and separation anxiety stage of her development. Susie would hoard her work, never allowing anyone to assist her for fear that she would look incompetent to her manager, even though this territorial attitude forced her to work very long hours and even weekends. To Susie, the more she took on her desk that others did not know how to do, the more secure she thought her position would be in the company.

Susie refused to train anyone on her desk, preferring to cement her value to the company being the only person capable of doing her tasks. Susie would continually volunteer herself for more projects and tasks to build her repertoire of expertise she just knew the company would not be able to do without.
Susie's anxiety and warped sense of importance resulted in a trip to the emergency room with an immediate resignation to her boss via email. She had to follow doctor's orders and seek another environment that she could feel secure in once again.

Chapter 3
Twelve Months And Showing Apprehension Around Strangers

Aimee Sassie at twelve months old was not very happy in a walker, playpen or infant swing at this age. She wanted to be free to play peek-a-boo, kick, wiggle and have all the freedom to walk around. Walking was her new accomplished milestone. The next adventure for her was always right around the corner. She would glow with a big smile when introduced by her name to a new person. She seemed to have a natural desire to make friends. Aimee wanted to look, feel and even touch this new stranger. It worked out really well if the new person approached her slowly with a warm smile. She needed a sense of security to get to know this new person, an affirmation that this new person, a stranger, was okay. (This was always the case unless Mommy wasn't around to make her environment safe.)

Aimee Sassie's instinct at twelve months of age that required her to feel a sense of security around a stranger did not change as she grew and entered the adult workforce. She joined Corporate America at the tender age of twenty-two. The world and the job were her zone. She was a hardworking student and had joined all the appropriate academic and associate groups in college that would reflect positively on her resume after graduation. After all, she had attended Harvard University. She was an Ivy League graduate that could take on the world of strangers.

She took her Harvard degree in Business with a minor in Human Resources Management and joined the ranks of a fortune 500 company. She joined the management team as Regional Human Resources Manager. This position would take her to new places with new faces. This was her dream coming true. She just beamed thinking about all of the opportunity!

Aimee's first year on the job was a whirlwind experience. She was introduced to multiple key leaders within the company. She was welcomed by scores of people that would introduce her to the details of success she desired and had worked so hard to accomplish with her studies in college. She spent her nights learning all the names and titles on the organizational charts. It was very important to Aimee to win the loyalty and approval of the people in business that could provide her with a sense of security and accomplishment.

As Aimee's career progressed, she became very good at her job. Professionals in the company respected her. The once strangers were now her mentors and felt like friends. At times, the people that she spent sixty hours a week with also felt like family.

Aimee Sassie was happy with her choice of careers and new family circle. She learned that there is no substitute for tackling a project with feverish determination and meeting the challenge at hand. She gained a wealth of knowledge from those in her path that had already taken a walk down the road of accomplishment.

Chapter 4
I'm Two And Can Play Make-Believe!

How many times as a Mom or Dad have you heard or used the phrase, "The Terrible Two's"? How about "The Wonderful Two's"? Both are very popular depending on what day of the week it is and how much sleep you were entitled to the night before. Remember.... I'm two and can play make believe but I'm very demanding!

As a two-year old child, Abbey Nosie was so curious and had an enormous imagination to tag along with it. "Look Mommy I'm a Dragon!" or "Look Daddy, I can fly!" This was also the age when Abbey developed a sense of self-awareness. How important am I? What can I do? What happens if I do this? The imagination of a two-year-old is endless and appears without boundaries to the tyke. The world can be whatever you make it and you can make a Zillion-kA- billion dollars, too!

In Corporate American, a Zillion-kA-billion dollars is the whole ball of wax. It is our image of success. It allows a lavish and rich lifestyle. The title given and sequence of zero's on the paycheck represent power and who you are to some people. Executives often display the same characteristics of a two-year-old in the boardroom trying to succeed and be the leader in this imaginary game of success. Once again we think of "The Terrible Two's" and "the Wonderful Two's". Now, it's story time...

It is Monday, 10:00 a.m. sharp and time for the executives to gather around the table and discuss business. The coffee is hot and so is the item on the agenda for today. (There is an enormous selection of donuts on the table. Chocolate, powered, glazed and Bear Claws!) The esteemed leaders must downsize the company. <u>They have to make people go away.</u> The leaders are supplied with yellow highlighters, red pens, organizational charts and calculators.

The leaders, one by one, highlight, circle boxes and discuss those staff members they deem to be non-essential to the company of the future. The calculator confirms the numbers. The donuts disappear from the table. It is a game of make believe in figuring out who "The Dragon" must slay and dispose of before time runs out. The leaders must continue "to fly" and keep the company soaring! The reduction must be quick.

" Remember, it's not personal, it's business,"... "The remaining employees will thank us for our wise decision," ..."It is our responsibility to make the tough decisions"; and "It's the bottom line that counts". "Collateral damage is expected during time of war". These are the thoughts in the minds of the leaders.

Now, that's imagination!

Chapter 5
Yes I'm Three

The <u>Who, What, When, Where and How</u> of life is usually understood by the three year old. The questions begin early in the morning and don't end until the active one is asleep for the night. Now that walking, running and playing is easy, it is time to work on understanding and using language in the world. This is the child's way of establishing a sense of independence. It is the beginning of making choices, learning to trust one's self and to develop a sense of initiative for one's self. "Me do it!" is written in more than one parent's journal. The young child understands the basic meaning of the words, now, soon and later. (And many more). This is also a time when the child loves to imitate and model behaviors of those adults who occupy their small world.

Matthew Conscious, a Payroll and Benefits Specialist for a medical facility with three thousand employees, often struggled with meeting assigned deadlines. He was an organized individual that made task list and his desk was neat. In general, it appeared that he had better than average time management skills; so, his boss was puzzled as to why Matthew often needed project deadlines extended. He was a shy yet articulate man. Matthew's words were few but wise.

One afternoon, Hilda Helper, the Director of Human Resources asked Matthew to step into her office. She needed to know the status of a benefits project that had been assigned to him three

Corporate America's Misbehaving Children

weeks earlier. Hilda had been Matthew's boss for three years and she traveled a great deal; so, a meeting was a rare occasion. The majority of their correspondence was by telephone or email.

Matthew took a seat and proceeded to take out his palm pilot while his boss finished a telephone call. Hilda completed her call and asked how Matthew was doing. He said "Great". Hilda asked Matthew if he had completed the benefits analysis report she had requested. Matthew said that he had several difficulties with the last payroll and would have it to her by the end of the day if that were okay. Hilda agreed but was not happy with yet another deadline missed by this staff member. Throughout the day, Hilda thought about what she could do to assist this employee. She was sure that Matthew's continued employment would be in jeopardy if his current job performance did not improve in this area.

The next day, Hilda reviewed the analysis and was pleased with the work. Once again she asked Matthew to step into her office. She told him that she was concerned about his inability to meet project deadlines and this was a warning that he had to focus on that objective. Matthew started to cry and beat his fist on the desk. This shy yet articulate man could not speak. The crying quickly turned to anger towards Hilda. He began to yell and call her obscene names. Hilda did not understand where this rage was coming from and tried to call security. Matthew pulled the phone from her arm! Hilda screamed and Matthew ran out of the building. This scene of violence lasted only minutes but seemed like hours to Hilda. After such a shocking ordeal, Hilda began her weekend early with rest and contemplation.

On Monday morning, after two sleepless nights of wondering how she had missed the signs of an employee in such trouble. She had many years' experience in Human Resources. She had begun her career as a Benefits Coordinator and was more than familiar with an Employee Assistance Program which she had tried unsuccessfully to have included in her company's employee benefit package. Matthew was a prime candidate for this type of program.

At noon, Hilda was in her office working when Matthew walked in, pulled the trigger and took Hilda's life. Matthew than turned the gun on himself and completed his own ultimate destruction.

Matthew like a three-year-old who did not realize that *soon* would eventually come, that *now* would not last forever and *later* was not acceptable as another of his delay tactics. Matthew did not learn that the world could be a safe place for him.

The CEO of this company had declined Hilda's proposal for an Employee Assistance Program three-year's in a row because of the cost to the bottom line. The CEO's "later" quickly became a "now", but not "soon" enough for Hilda.

The three year old loves to imitate those actions and behaviors that have been seen as bringing rewards. They will copy the dress, mannerisms, personality and other behavior traits of their parents, siblings, peers, teachers, etc. The parent of a three year old must have coined the phrase, "Monkey See, Monkey Do". It seems to be the way a small child learns how to act and act out. This can be of a positive or negative nature. This new feeling of self-ruling allows a child to learn to be confident. The ability to try new things and make decisions allows for the growth of faith and trust in one's self. It is of course, a life-long learning experience of continuing to evolve one's personality and socialization skills. Unfortunately for some, this mimicking behavior continues on into the working world and the person chosen, as their "mentor", is not always the type of team member desired by fellow employees and managers.

Kasey Kong focused his behavior to mimicking his manager, Harry King, who gave all the outward signs of being highly successful in his position and moving on the fast track. He had only been with the company for two years and Kasey noticed how other managers and employees would always speak to him and extend gracious amenities when they came into contact with Harry. Harry's management style was to micro-manage all in his area of responsibility, continually demean his staff's performance in front of others, and always want to call them on something in meetings with others present. Harry reveled in making the employee feel totally incompetent and self-doubting by questioning every idea or solution they would represent. Kasey naturally assumed that if he aped this same behavior, he would also be noticed by the powers that be and would move up the corporate ladder quickly on the backs of others, just like Harry. What Kasey did not know was that Harry had offended so many of his staff and employees from other departments that the executive level was working on how to move him out of the company with the least negative consequences to overall production.

Kasey even took on the mannerisms of Harry when he walked through the office and participated in staff meetings. He would question the other staff in the meeting in ways that were intended to make them look foolish and incompetent, to gain Harry's attention and admiration. Harry loved it. Kasey was like a protégé to him and Harry was very proud that someone would want to imitate his management style. After all, Harry's style produced results in his department.

You can imagine Kasey's shock when he was terminated the same day that Harry was asked to resign. He had fallen victim to tying his future to one manager instead of developing his own management style after conscious observance of what style worked best in the culture of the company he was a part of and then adapting his own personal management style for success.

Chapter 6
What Is Real And What Is Imaginary At Four

The ever-developing four-year-old may still be bossy in personality, like to play games and change the rules on a whim. It is also a task to learn the difference between what is real and is imaginary as child's play continues at a feverish pace.

In the name of fun, they decide for themselves and their friends that they should jump rope first since they are the more cute or handsome one in the group. In fact, they have decided that only the better-looking ones get to have a turn at all. In their world of play, only certain people matter. The most important is that they win the game.

Caroline believes that her rules of the game are the best. She gets to decide who, what, when or where the game is played and how for that matter. This is an attitude that Caroline keeps, as she grows into a school age child, adolescent, teenager then an adult. The adult Caroline believes that her rules of the game are better than her co-workers in the business. In her imaginary world, she is still the cutest and therefore is entitled to make the decisions for herself as well as those around her. She is the ruler of the corner office. She has the leading box on the organizational chart in the Marketing department.

Caroline rules the Marketing department with her ideals. She decides what projects are necessary and will score her some value points with the CEO. All decisions are made with her opinion and what she believes is best. A bossy attitude and a snide remark are the plan for dealing with most people who disagree with her. In this imaginary world, she is the most important person at all times and this must be respected. In reality, her co-workers and the people who call her "boss" laugh and make jokes about her self-centeredness. It is a well-known fact to colleagues and the people that she supervises that she will drop kick to someone else to finish a project. She often disappears with a personal plan during the true office crisis. Caroline is also so foolish as to take complete credit for the work of others. She truly believes that she is respected and admired by her colleagues.

The sad reality of Caroline's behavior in the workplace is that she never learned to identify between reality and her imagination. She failed to discover that respect in management is often measured through perseverance, consistency and the integrity of one's word. It was not uncommon for Caroline to promise an employee to support an idea to the CEO then cowardly change her mind on a whim in the boardroom when the CEO did not offer support for an idea. Caroline's reaction was to remain quiet and neutral. The final outcome would be that Caroline would agree with whatever the CEO decided. She would remain silent and wait to see how she could win at this table. After years of this behavior in meetings with the CEO, it was no wonder that Caroline's colleagues and her staff did not trust her. She was not genuine towards them. Caroline was nothing more than a Marketing Director without a real plan and viewed as an untrustworthy liar who would do anything to further her own agenda. This was the reality of the situation.

Savannah Swift studied to be an Engineer in college and worked for five years in the field until she realized that the secluded world of calculations and precise figures did not allow her to exercise a perceived gift for communications. Savannah enjoyed the challenge of finding ways to make the company more efficient. It was a joy to create a new product that would create thousands in revenue for her employer. She knew it would also benefit her wallet. However at the end of the day when she arrived home, she felt a sense of loss, a sensation of being disconnected from others. She loved numbers yet she also loved people. She enjoyed listening to the company gossip. Savannah often gave the impression in the office that she was all business and only cared about the success of the accounting department. In actuality, she was famished for friendship and lived vicariously through the lives of others. Being of a soft heart, she would cry easily and truly cared about other people. She often appeared tormented as she pretended not to care about others in the presence of her superiors although, she had mastered the ability to put on "a poker face" and talk business. She learned to cry later in the shadows.

Savannah became a friend with the Director of Public Relations since this allowed Savannah to know what was happening in the company to a degree and feel connected to the people in the organization. It allowed her a feeling of superiority to know the financial scoop at all times plus the personal details of the employees. By appearances, the two were good friends, could share office secrets and covered each other's back with the boss.

This office friendship lasted for years until one day; the Director of Public Relations was no longer with the company. Savannah had to make a decision whether to continue her friendship with this person or cut the ties since this person was no longer with the company. Sadly, Savannah said her Good Bye by email correspondence and never spoke with her friend again.

The friend realized in the weeks to come that Savannah was never really a true friend to her, only a messenger of information. All of the conversations at lunch that were supposed to be between comrades were stored up in Savannah's mind to use when needed to further her career. The many tears that she shed were only to gain trust.

This was a lesson for the unemployed Director of Public Relations that in the savvy world of business, keep it about profit and never make it personal. It will break your heart... if you still have one, and will leave you wondering what was real.

Corporate America's Misbehaving Children

Chapter 7
Inventing Games And Rules

It must be a special gift to be employed as a Kindergarten teacher. The teacher is the extended parent for the school day of six hours for anywhere from fifteen to twenty five year olds. For some of the students, it is the first experience away from Mom and Dad. It may also be the first experience of being separated from siblings. The Kindergarten teacher is trusted with the most distinguished gifts in the human race. This unique person will have the job of teaching the young ones the most basic skills of following simple rules among other important social and academic skills that will be needed as the child grows to adulthood. The five-year-old will naturally do his and her part to invent games in the classroom and on the playground to exercise creativity and extend the definition of play.

The challenge of inventing a game for Justin Dare was a simple and fun task. He was especially happy if it meant that he and his friends could use matchbox cars. Justin and his buddies (Charlie, Kade, Cameron and Jason) only needed dirt and imagination to accomplish this goal. It's just five little boys having a good time!

In the adult world of business the challenge of inventing a game with simple rules is often referred to as a plan of action or business plan and the rules are anything but simple! The only player in the game that believes the rules are simple must be walking around with blinders or be a recent college graduate.

Aggression, strategy and competition replace the innocence of the five-year-old.

In Corporate America, the game is always a strategic event that requires planning and research. The object of the game is to be first, remain a player and win. You must always be one step ahead of the person next to you. There is no true code of conduct in this game. The players are not your friends. The player who bounces back and forth with the power will remain in the game the longest. The player who is concerned about employee ideas, internal and external perceptions or other sociological factors is eliminated from the game. The major players will tell you, "I'll take my chances". The recent college graduate may be foolish enough to say, "I just want to stay in the game". Regardless, you have winners and losers.

Tommy Tops could be described by the boss as the "Number 1 Player" in the laboratory of a small southern hospital. He volunteers for the graveyard shift and never complains. He always works the holiday schedule since he is a single gentleman with no family obligations. Tommy is the person who understands a single mother needs to be off fifteen minutes early to take a sick child to the doctor and covers his co-worker's duties. He is confident in his aspirations and goals for success. He understands that he does not have to bamboozle a co-worker to get ahead in the game. He is truly a rare item in the workplace.

Brad Bomber is the exact opposite of Tommy Tops. He is every manager's "high-need" employee. He is fifteen minutes late each day and cannot make it to a meeting on time even with the assistance of a palm pilot alarm. Brad prides himself on being the eldest son of a millionaire and therefore does very little work. He believes his social status allows him to ride on the coattails of his co-workers. The other reporters at the station do not respect his writing and laugh at his constant whining about story assignments. He has not conceded to the theory that hard work pays off. Brad believes that since his father worked seventy hours per week, seven days per week, it is sufficient to cover his career as well. He is self-absorbed to the point that he cannot see that all who makes his acquaintance for five minutes despises him. If only, he could job shadow Tommy Tops.

Chapter 8
Six And Venturing Out

The six year old has been in school through kindergarten and first grade and beginning to really enjoy the independence from the safe harbor of home and parents. They have made new friends and identify with other children who share the same likes and dislikes. They must have the same friends in order to belong. The children compete very hard among themselves to have the teacher like them best.

The professional child has now been in the corporate environment for a couple of years and is ready to test their independence further, align themselves with the appropriate group of friends, those who can help advance their own personal agendas and agree with everything they do, and assert themselves to make sure that their teacher is aware that they exist. At this stage in the employee's career path, they work very hard to be the Teacher's (Boss's) Pet. They spend a lot of time and energy trying to make sure the boss knows who is doing what at all times. Take little Charlie Kissup for example, small in stature but large in arrogance and self-admiration.

When Charlie Kissup joined the company as a staff accountant, he was personally walked around the office and introduced to everyone by the Chief Operating Officer, Dennis. This act in itself elevated Charlie in his own mind immediately to a place in the overall company much higher than his position represented.

Dennis had even hired Charlie outside of the normal channels and company procedures used for all other new hires. Charlie was allowed to by-pass taking any of the required pre-employment tests that all other applicants had to take and pass, prior to being considered for employment. Dennis hired Charlie on his own and then brought him to the office on a Monday morning strutting him around like a "debutant coming out" presentation to the office staff. Dennis either did not think of or care that his action was placing the company at risk for treating the young man different from the other applicants. The company had failed to hire other applicants in protected classes because they could not pass the required pre-employment tests. Dennis was only concerned and focused on what he wanted and he wanted Charlie Kissup.

Charlie knew he was Dennis's admired one and never failed to flaunt it. His elevated self-worth did not win him many friends in the office, but then Charlie was not concerned because he had tied himself to one of the Big Bosses and believed the world was his for the plucking.

Charlie never failed to thrust his special status in everyone's face, even those is higher positions in the organization than his. On more than one occasion, when Charlie would learn of an error by someone in the office, he would leave skid marks from his desk to Dennis's office in the executive wing. Dennis would reinforce this treacherous behavior by listening and then patting Charlie on the head and thanking him as he would send him on his way. Now Dennis would lay in wait like a saber tooth tiger in the bushes for the employee who had made the error. If the employee did not immediately come forward, Dennis would pounce without mercy in the presence of others. Charlie would smirk and move on to the next victim to use to secure his "teacher's pet" position. Most employees in the office, aware of his agenda, would just try and keep contact with him at a minimum and look toward the day when Dennis would move on to another company, leaving Charlie Kissup behind for them to deal with - and they would deal with him.

Doesn't every company appear to have an office version of Dennis and Charlie Kissup? It can be a small, medium or large company, any industry and there is always someone with a childish behavior. The most unfortunate of this situation is that most employees with this "inner six-year-old" are recognized as high achievers in the business arena. It is the CEO who doesn't care about the employees, only the profit that is shown to stockholders. It is the Board of Directors that would sell their "Mother's wedding gown" to the highest bidder if it acknowledged them in the press. It is the Office Clerk who pretends to be kind to everyone and always willing to help out a co-worker who can tell a lie with a straight face. It is the Comptroller who is secretly embezzling thousands of dollars from the company.

Our Dennis and Charlie lurk behind every desk, on every floor and at numerous levels masked as a "Company Star, Employee of the Month or Most Dedicated Employee". Unfortunately, the only difference between a first grader trying to be the "Teacher's Pet" and the employee trying to be "Employee of the Month" is that one of them should be old enough not to allow the inner child to play these menacing games in a business environment.

Chapter 9
Developing an Awareness of Time and Money at Seven

Will you be my best friend? I'll give you $5 dollars! Boys are gross! Girls are gross! My brother can run faster than your brother can! My house is cool! Your car is ugly! My Dad makes more money than your Dad does! You're trailer trash! She's rich!

These are only a few of the comments that you might hear if you listen to a group of seven-year-old boys and girls. The world of the seven-year-old is viewed as black and white, good or bad and nothing is in between! You are either the best friend or the enemy. It is a journey of finding criticism fun and difficult at the same time.

Frances Frugal was an outgoing, happy yet awkward girl in the second grade. She had long legs, long arms and the children teased her because she lived in a small blue trailer house. She was an only child that didn't seem to notice that her house was small and different than her friends. Frances appeared as an average second grader but she had the eyes of a much older child. She seemed to have wisdom beyond her years. The teachers at school always complimented her for making good grades. She enjoyed this praise.

Corporate America's Misbehaving Children

As a young girl, Frances understood that her parents did not have much money and she needed to be conservative with her allowance. She knew that she couldn't buy candy at school and have coins for the ice cream truck on the weekend. Frances was given coins at the beginning of the week and guarded them in a small pink purse. One Sunday afternoon, the ice cream truck came down the street. Frances heard it from inside her bedroom and quickly grabbed her pink purse. As Frances slammed the door and ran towards the street, she had not zipped her purse and the few coins fell out. Frances quickly tried to find all of her coins in the grass. She found all but one penny. Frances searched and searched but never found the one more penny that she needed to buy an ice cream sandwich. She began to cry and ran to her father to ask for another penny. Sadly, her father opened out his pockets and they were empty. The family was broke until the first of the month. Frances cried herself to sleep that night.

This lesson was tough for a second grader who was just starting to learn the value of money. As the years passed, Frances made a vow to herself that she would get a good education and a good job. She understood that children teased her because she had very little money, toys or even a nice house. She remembers the other children laughing because her dresses were too short for her long legs and her shoes were dirty.

Today, Frances is a middle-aged woman who works hard to stay ahead in an often cold, calculating and competitive business world. She never forgot the vow. She studied very hard in school, made good grades, went to college on a scholarship and graduated. The awareness of little money and hard times as a child created a strong work ethic in Frances. She married a wonderful man who also works very hard to provide for his family and her children will never know the pain of loosing that all important penny.

This strong work ethic and desire to have enough money for "beyond the basics" is what keeps Frances motivated to stay in the corporate world. As an adult, she understands that the playing field is not level for children or adults in this world. She understands that some employees in a job receive favor for being; while others, must work ten and twelve hours per day to survive the corporate machine. She has accepted that name calling and ruthless competition do not end when you're a second grader. She prays for the day when time and money are not direct opponents in the corporate world.

Chapter 10
At Eight, We Love To Share Stories

Several words come to mind when we think of an eight-year-old child: trusting, innocent, sweet, friendly, obedient, carefree, appreciative and vibrant. It is a time in which a child becomes a natural storyteller. The subject at hand is one's self since they don't have very much experience to tell about other people. The stories are told with an excitement beyond words and come with wonderful facial expressions as the eight-year-old is still in a time of innocence. The imagination is pure and inventive in nature.

Madeleine Minute's career had been a wild roller coaster ride in the field of Cosmetics and Beauty. From a very young age, Madeleine loved to shampoo hair and make you pretty. She would tell you stories about her childhood while painting your nails. She loved to share stories of her grandmother who was "Second Mom" to her. One could say that she was a carefree adult that never lost the spirit of the eight-year-old.

As a result of her sense of sweetness and appreciation for life, the business world often seemed harsh to Madeleine. She just loved to create beauty and make people feel loved. This was of course a trait she inherited from her grandmother. She often hopped from one job to another to escape the numbers side of the beauty business. It was difficult for her to find the obedience needed to build a clientele of customers from salon to salon. It was hurtful to Madeleine to be told that she did a wonderful cut and style but needed to bring in more new clients to the business or she would need to give up her station in the beauty shop. She could not understand economics. She could not understand that telling stories about her life and family were considered negative in the business world.

After ten years of changing jobs and experiencing the same result, Madeleine decided to open her own business. She decided to live by the minute as her last name portrayed. She created a salon with a sense of style and fun. It was decorated with floral benches and tables that encouraged her customers to have a seat, grab a cup of coffee and tell their own stories. She had hanging plants in every corner of the shop. Madeleine's love for living plants was also nurtured by the time she spent with her grandmother.

This change of mission became a financial windfall for Madeleine. In no time at all, her little beauty shop was featured in many newspapers and her clientele was booming. Today, Madeleine owns a chain of successful beauty salons.

Chapter 11
The Nine-Year Old Bully

By the age of nine, if a child is going to take on the characteristics of being an aggressive bully, it usually has shown itself by now. Every school has at least one bully and very often there is one at each grade level with one in particular being the biggest bully in the entire school. Most employees have encountered this type of personality in their organization. It is not uncommon for a company to have a bully in each of its many levels with one that stands above the others. In most cases, this bully of bullies is in one of the senior levels of the company and the bullies in training below will try and model this behavior among their peers in the lower ranks. The bullies in the lower management levels do not usually last long. They create havoc, require too much maintenance, and their libelous behavior is not neutralized by the value they are perceived as bringing to the organization. The more you can help the bottom line of an organization, the more you are forgiven for your unacceptable behaviors. The top bullies can mistreat others as long as their services continue to impact the bottom line positively.

Karl Max was a master at bullying all who worked with or for him. And the saddest behavior attribute that Karl demonstrated was the joy he seemed to experience from watching his victims fall prey to his cruel treatment.

Karl was brought into the financially challenged company with the task to put it back into a profitable situation. The company was loosing a million dollars a month and the investors were applying pressure to the President to either turn it around or they would take appropriate measures to cut their investment loses. The President wooed Karl for many months before Karl finally agreed to come on board and do what he could to save the organization. From his first day of employment, Karl had enormous power over the company's activities, direction and employees. Most employees thought that Karl's power and direction came directly from the investor group. No organizational level or employee position was excluded from the power bestowed upon him, including the President. Karl was keenly aware of the power he had over others and flaunted this superior position consistently and aggressively.

Heads began to roll in the upper ranks of several company divisions within the first couple of months. Karl worked down the organizational ladder and sliced and diced the employee ranks viciously his first year. Department managers were not allowed to fill many of the resulting vacant employee positions and those positions that were filled had to be filled with applicants who would accept compensation below their market value. Managers and department heads had to do the same amount of work or more with fewer and fewer employees or with employees with lower skills based on the salaries they were authorized to pay these new employees. Workdays became twelve and fourteen hours long consistently but no one dared to complain unless they were also ready to be unemployed. Karl had put the fear in all remaining employees.

To feed and maintain Karl's appetite to stay and continue with his turn-around project, he was given larger and larger bonuses with the funds made available from cutting positions and salaries of the employees and line managers. Only Karl and other executives reaped these large bonus rewards. The "worker bees" were just considered lucky to have employment and the raping of their hard work and sweat continued.

Karl was proud of his battlefield wins and bragged about his ability to intimidate others. On occasions when Karl and any of his managers would discuss a problem one of the managers was having with a vendor or peer, Karl would be sure and tell his staff managers to feel free to use his name to make things happen. Most managers, however, did not take Karl up on this intimidation by proxy offer.

As the career ladder is climbed, a top bully gets very bored. It did not take very long for Karl to become bored with his group. This man-child's ego required more, more, more! He had to feel superior regardless of circumstance (a true bully trait).

On a regular basis, Karl would contemplate his next victim. The little nine-year-old freckled face tyrant that still existed within his black soul of a man was always contemplating his next victim.

Employees were much like small fish to this man. The corporate office was his aquarium. He was the Great White Shark swimming around waiting to devour his next meal. One by one, the tank becomes empty then is replaced with new, younger and unprepared fish. This new variety is exciting to Karl and the cycle of bullying and devouring begins again.

Marjorie Wooster & Sandra Simoneaux

Chapter 12
Ten And Challenging Parental Authority & Society Rules

As the parent of a "tweener" and a "teenager", I look back fondly on the joyous moments shared with a ten year old. Your child is independent yet not sassy, yet. Your ten-year-old enjoys being your friend and it's still okay to be Mom. It is an age that you don't realize that being a parent is to be treasured. Your son or daughter feels comfortable making new friends, still likes to give Mom and Dad a hug, and enjoys planning and taking part in outings with you. It is the time for beginning debates and the love of trivia. The ten-year-old understands cause and effect. It is the beginning of challenging your parental authority and house rules.

Unfortunately, the beginning of challenging authority does not end for some with the coming of age. Many young adults at eighteen, nineteen and beyond continue to challenge parental authority and society's rules. In fact, it is not uncommon to view this "challenge of authority" in the office with employees who are well past the formative years. Behavior that may be considered charming by a ten year old is anything but cute at thirty-two years of age. In fact, most employers consider challenging authority as just plain rude and a reason for termination. The employee handbook will more than likely refer to this type of behavior as insubordinate and reason for termination.

Rhonda Whiner, a recent college graduate was afforded her first opportunity in Corporate America as a Database Coordinator for a public company. Rhonda, became one of 3,000 employees in this massive corporate think tank. She wore her employee badge with pride yet often questioned the Human Resources Department as to why certain policies were written as such. At first, the Human Resources Department viewed Rhonda's steady questions as part of her orientation to the company. After six months of employment, Rhonda continued to drop by the Human Resources Department with yet another question. Better yet, she would leave long detailed voice message explanations for the Human Resource Staff as to why she felt a policy should be changed. Rhonda was relentless with her questions. Eventually, Rhonda's messages became annoying and childish to the point of the just ignoring them.

Once Rhonda realized that the Human Resources staff no longer wished to explain policy to her or hear her recommendations for change, she finally moved her need to challenge authority to her immediate boss in the Information Systems Department.

Arthur Strict, Director of Information Systems (IS), was a very precise, organized and analytical boss who never worked less than twelve hours per day. Arthur worked hard to have his IS department always teetering on the cutting edge of technology. After all, he had paid his dues as a programmer for many years and was still spending his weekends at his desk.

One day, Rhonda requested to meet with Arthur after a department meeting. Rhonda walked into his office armed with the policy manual and a list of notes. The list of notes were her documented conversations with the Human Resources department on not one but all thirty- seven company policies. Arthur, being the exact thinker that he was smiled and listened as Rhonda proceeded to run down her list of negative comments one by one with her boss. It was an exercise of patience for Arthur as he continued to listen to her. After forty-five minutes, Arthur kindly told her that he had a meeting and they would need to discuss her concerns at another time. Rhonda continued to read from her list. Arthur just stood up and said, "Thank You." At this point, Rhonda got the message to leave his office.

After two weeks, Rhonda became more frustrated that Arthur had not replied to her emails requesting another meeting. So, Rhonda decided it was time to take her opinion of the policies to a higher source of power in the organization. Next, Rhonda requested to meet with the Chief Financial Officer (CFO), Randolph Peck. Randolph Peck in this company was in charge of multiple departments including Information Systems.

Randolph was well known in the company as a sharp, determined and quick to action type person. He was results-oriented. Mr. Peck was also known to "cut to the chase" on matters as time was of the essence in all matters.

Reluctantly, Mr. Peck agreed to meet with Rhonda for fifteen minutes on a Friday afternoon. Rhonda was delighted and once again came armed with her notebook of complaints into his office. As before, Rhonda began complaining and arguing that the policies of the company should be this way and that way. She became very excited and argumentative and said that she was tired of having to deal with "no action" from top management on her concerns. Mr. Peck very calmly stood up after eleven minutes into Rhonda's incessant squealing and told her that she needed to take the weekend to consider if she still wished to remain employed with the company since obviously she was dissatisfied with so many areas in the company.

Rhonda exited Mr. Peck's office with a blank and astonished look on her face. What had she done wrong? Did he just fire her? Rhonda did not understand that she had taken her questions to a level that was considered insubordination. She had neglected her job trying to prove that someone else had not done his or her job in Human Resources. By challenging the Human Resources Department, her immediate boss and finally the CFO, Rhonda had crossed the corporate chain of command line. She had crossed the line of challenging the corporate parental authority and was sent to time-out to consider her behavior and the consequences.

Billy Butte managed the Administration Department, which included Human Resources Information Systems (HRIS) and payroll. Billy had over fifteen years experience in these areas with topnotch expertise. What Billy also had was an unrealistic view of his importance. Billy would interrupt and challenge anyone who would offer suggestions or new ideas on how to process payroll or HRIS reports to improve efficiencies, especially if the input came from his or another manager. No one knew as much as he did about his areas of responsibility. Billy did not care where or in whose presence he was in when he became defensive and would shoot down suggestions from others on how to improve the products and service his department was responsible for. In staff meetings with his supervisor and his peer managers, Billy's posture in these meetings was always very stiff and erect, giving the impression that he was ready to pounce on anyone's comments or suggestions involving his department. He would not allow himself to even entertain the thought that his manager or any manager knew as much or more than he about HRIS or payroll. Billy never considered that everyone benefits from pooling information and brainstorming meetings where some of the greatest ideas are generated. "Synergy" was not in Billy's vocabulary or field of understanding. Billy challenged and defied his manager's suggestions to adopt new processes one too many times.

Chapter 13
The Need To Know And Understand Everything At Eleven!

Any parent can visit the local library or the internet and find scores of information about how an 11-year-old will act on a regular basis. Your son or daughter has a better understanding of money and what it will buy. A child has a need to know why and understand thought processes. Your child selects friends based on mutual interests. He or she may be argumentative, moody and sensitive. Your child needs privacy. Peers are more important than parents and they are starting to think about possible jobs of the future at this age.

Cindy Crash works very hard at her Operations job for a small manufacturer. She arrives early to review items on the production floor for quality, color and style accuracy. Cindy is a perfectionist with a "get it done" attitude. She begins her day with happiness and guarded optimism. She works through each moment of the day solving problems with product, staff and senior management.

Cindy's career with this company began while she was still in high school. She worked part-time, then full-time and with each year of experience gained more confidence in her abilities. She also reaped the benefits of moving up the management ladder at a young age. She is every employer's dream. Cindy handles whatever needs to be handled throughout the course of the business day from physical labor to production cost analysis to marketing planners. She is a thirty-year-old woman now and knows her craft as no other in the industry.

This grown woman often asks herself the same things at this age as she did when she was thinking as an eleven-year-old preteen. Why are things done this way? Where is the money spent? Why is the money spent this way? Why does my boss require all of my time? Why does my boss want to be my friend? Why can't my boss respect that I have a life outside the business world? What happens tomorrow? Will this job be here next year? Will this company continue to employ me?

Cindy is so intelligent and high-spirited that she demands to know her future with this company. She wants to know if senior management appreciates her contributions. She wants to know why she works harder than some of her co-workers yet they reap similar or better job perks. The list of questions and concerns grows with each forty, fifty or sixty hour week and every passing year.

As any employee, she wonders if the company will remain in business. What will she do if the company is sold or dissolved? Cindy finds herself torn between what is comfortable, routine and has always been her life. She struggles with the concept of going to college on a full-time basis and giving up her job. She is consumed with gratitude towards senior management for teaching her business yet cannot quench the desire to reach out for something different.

Cindy is an example of the employee of the past, the present and the future. She doesn't mean to distrust and question her employer. She doesn't mean to think like an eleven-year-old girl. Although, she knows that her pink slip can come at any point in her career without warning and due to no fault by her, it could just be a business decision motivated by the bottom line.

Chapter 14
How Do I look?

How do I look? This is a question that seems to occupy the mind of the twelve-year-old. At this stage of development, social interaction with peers and the perception of how we appear to others is paramount in the mind of the pre-teen. It is a time of transitioning from primary school to junior high. These are difficult years for the pre-teen as physical and mental maturation is in full bloom. Our little girl or boy is changing in physical appearance and it is difficult to cope with all of the changes that introduces he or she to adolescence. This is without a doubt, a true time of questions about self and others that are endless for a parent.

Our "tween" is self-absorbed with "How do I look?" It is an endless exchange between mother and daughter as to what is acceptable appearance and behavior. It is a time for fathers and sons to challenge one another's skill set in everything from sports to education in order to find the male acceptance mark in this world. Let us not forget that this is also an invitation for young people to question how the male and female coincide peacefully in an often-judgmental academic environment. These are the years that a parent begins to hear about peer groups at schools. The nerds, the jocks, the cheerleaders, the cool kids, the not cool kids, the "A" group, the "B" group. The list of social organization among the twelve-year-old is astounding to the average parent.

Corporate America's Misbehaving Children

The social organization experienced by the twelve-year-old is not very different from the social groups that exist in many business offices.

Hazel Habitte considered herself a corporate member of the "A" group. She pranced into the employee lounge every Monday morning proceeding to tell everyone about her weekend. She assumed that every detail of what she wore, where she went, whom she went with (or without) and how she spent her weekend was the highlight of those gathered at the coffeepot. She was polite and would ask about your weekend; however, prior to your response, she was on to her story. The details of ME!

Hazel was an expert at providing trivia, right down to the latest shade of hair color. It was quite amusing for the majority of the employees to wait for the "color" of the month. Jet black appeared to be her favorite; although, she did surprise everyone with a peroxide blonde effect during the summer months. One day a male co-worker of Hazel's commented that in the right shades of sunlight her hair looked purple. She smiled and said, "Thank You" as though this was truly meant as a compliment. Rumor has it they began an out of the office romance shortly after that encounter.

It was entertaining for the female co-workers to witness Hazel do her make-up in the ladies room for thirty minutes each day. One could only assume that she deducted this time from her lunch hour. She was so conscientious to share her latest beauty secret of finding a blush that accentuated her cheekbones. It was a mental hazard to listen to her clarify the different shades of pink blush.

Poor Hazel, she appeared to suffer from a low self-esteem disorder or perhaps she simply never matured beyond the mind of the twelve-year-old when it came to her looks.

Chapter 15
Pushing The Bar As A New Teenager

Reaching the age of thirteen for Tracie Challenge was a milestone for her. She was now referred to as a "teenager" and what a crown that is to wear. This was a transition period between childhood and dependence on others for meeting her needs and setting rules and the adult world where she would be totally responsible for herself and held accountable for her actions.

Sometimes it seemed like Tracie's only focus, like most thirteen year olds, was to see how far the bar could be pushed in compromising parental rules. She wanted to immediately take control of her life and make her own rules. As a new teenager, Tracie suddenly believed that she knew what was best for her much better than her parents.

As most thirteen year old adolescents defy their parents, break the rules and pay the consequences in these early teen years, they slowly begin to recognize and almost admit out loud that maybe their parents do know what is best at times and were not just trying to forcibly contain and control them, but to guide them through the bumps and hic-cups of life drawing from their own years of experiences to help them develop into mature responsible adults. And just maybe with this help, the teenager

Corporate America's Misbehaving Children

could learn some lessons without all of the pain involved when bad decisions are made impulsively.

In our years of human resources management in the corporate world, we have encountered many employees who unfortunately never came to this realization and continued to make their own rules of conduct and constantly rebelled against organizational rules, procedures and office etiquette.

Ben Ludan was the President of a newly acquired company. Even though the acquisition prevented Ben's company from falling into unrecoverable bankruptcy, he was not happy at the thought of his company now being just one of several subsidiaries of a larger conglomerate. This was still his company no matter what name it now went by and he would run it his way as he had always done. Ben could never accept any responsibility for his bad leadership and management style as being factors in the downfall of the company. It was the economic state of the nation, unskilled or lazy employees, unfair competition and any other factor he could dredge up to place the responsibility on. He threw darts of blame at everyone while he clothed himself in thick armor.

Ben refused to follow the new parent company's policies and procedures. When he decided that someone needed more compensation, Human Resources was never contacted for consultation on the position's salary range, the employee's performance or the company's compensation philosophy. Ben would approve substantial increases or promotions without providing any supporting data for justification. After all, if he approved the increase or promotion no one should question his action. Ben of course would inform the employee first of the increase or promotion and then forward the paperwork to Human Resources. When the Human Resources Director would call him to discuss the inappropriate increase or promotion, Ben would always just reply with, "Well, I have approved it and the employee has already been told, so it will have to stand as is".

Ben's managers would hire and terminate employees at will, never following the stated guidelines in the Manager's Handbook for these actions. The Human Resources Department was, as usual, the last to be informed of the employment action. Ben's attitude was prevalent among all of his managers, supervisors and staff throughout his subsidiary. The subsidiary was run by renegades led by Ben determined to maintain control. Even though the acquisition of Ben's company by a more stable organization ensured future existence and employment for him and his employees, Ben continually reacted as if it had been a hostile takeover.

The senior executives in the parent company appeared to be incapable of controlling him and his "storm trooper" managers. Only after a year went by and the subsidiary's income bottom line began to move to the red area did the parent company take steps to change the attitude and culture of the subsidiary. And as we all know, the culture of any company comes from the leaders at the top. Ben was summarily terminated, with a severance package most employees only dream about. Ben had pushed the bar until it could bend no farther and it snapped back on him.

Many company managers and executives perceive the prevailing employment laws as detriments to being able to conduct business in a profitable manner. These laws hinder their ability to do business, as they deem necessary to make a profit for themselves and their stockholders. These executives constantly weigh the risk of pushing the limit of the law. What are the odds that an employee will even know what the prevailing law is for their particular circumstance? Even corporate lawyers are unclear on how courts will rule on a particular incident or employment practice in their company. Different courts have been known to rule differently on identical situations. Case law is a moving target in the employment law world.

One area that is constantly being challenged in the courts is employee classification – exempt versus non-exempt status. The majority of the time, the issue is because the company classifies employees as exempt when their task and duties actually fall under non-exempt status. What is the motivating factor for wrongly classifying employees to exempt? No overtime wages! Companies can work exempt employees sixty hours a week and not have to compensate them with overtime pay. On the other side of the coin, employees are protected from having their pay

Corporate America's Misbehaving Children

docked if they miss time at work and do not have vacation, sick, or other paid time-off days to cover the lost hours.

The thought process under this law is that exempt employees are paid to do a job, not by the hour. The positions are usually professional in nature requiring a higher degree of education or professional certification. Many times these jobs will entail projects with deadlines that require more than eight hours a day or forty hours a week to complete. The intent of the law for exempt employees is to allow these positions more flexibility in their work hours and to also insulate them from exploitation by the employer. True, they are not compensated with overtime pay, however they are protected from having their pay reduced by hours they do not work in the workweek. This should be a win-win situation for employee and employer. However..............

Gary Garnish, was the President of a rapidly growing sales driven company. The largest group of employees in the company were producers and sales processors and they were classified as exempt. The fact that these positions actually worked at a desk every day, punched a time clock and never called on customers outside of the office did not matter. The company chose to classify them as sales because they would work long hours during the week and weekends to solicit business since their compensation was largely based on commissions from sales with a pittance monthly salary. Overtime pay for these employees would be substantial.

Mary Sharp had been with the company as a sales processor for three years. She was extremely conscientious about her desk responsibilities. She worked through her lunch most days and took work home at night and on the weekends if necessary. She was very happy with her position and the company because she felt valued for the extra time and work that she would give to produce above average results for the company. Management praised Mary for her quality production.

That is until Mary had more sickness in her family than usual and had to take time off to tend to her sick children or herself. When Mary ran out of sick leave in the fall of the year and took two days off because one of her children was sick, Gary Garnish decided to set her up as an example to others about taking too much time off. Gary was seeing problems with other employees in this area and decided that the time had come to let the employees know that abusing time off would not be tolerated, so he decided to reduce Mary's wages for the two days she was off. Mary was furious. What happened to all of the gratitude expressed before about the many hours she spent working nights and weekends without ever complaining about not getting overtime compensation for her efforts? Mary complained to her manager to no avail. Gary saved the company a few hours of overtime compensation costs, but what he did not realize was that he was in the process of losing one of his best employees in mind, body and spirit. Who do you think the real winner was? Instead of win-win this resulted in a lose-lose situation.

Corporate America's Misbehaving Children

Chapter 16
The World Revolves Around Only Me

Narcissism becomes the dominant trait for many adolescents and rules most fourteen and fifteen year olds. The most troubling aspect of this adolescent thought process to the parent is that the teenager truly believes that the world does revolve around them and only them. Why wouldn't they think that? After all, they are so beautiful and intelligent at this stage. Sadly, some of these adolescents never quite grow up and out of this narcissistic stage. Maturity escapes them and they enter into the corporate world with the same self-centered and self-absorbing attitudes.

Doris Honey oozed with this attitude. Of course, the fact that she was the girlfriend of one of the company's senior executives and held an executive position in the company only reinforced her high standing in the company pecking order. And naturally, being the goddess she was, there were no limits to her abuse of power, even among the other managers and executives. When she made a request to employees, it was just understood that if her request was not moved to the top of the employee's task priority list, then that employee would most likely be the object of her "pillow talk" that night and no one wanted to be the subject of Doris's "pillow talk".

Doris was a thirty-five year old tall, lean, bleached blonde who always violated the company dress code with skirts that were barely three inches below her panty line. Her choice of lipstick color was hot pink and hair color was strawberry blonde, styled in the famous 1960's football helmet coiffure.

When Doris sat in a chair, she never crossed or closed her legs, giving a full frontal view to anyone who was unfortunate enough to be meeting with her. It did not matter to Doris if the audience was male or female or large or small. Her dress code violations were brought to the attention of other managers and executives on numerous occasions, including the Senior Human Resources Manager because of the many employee complaints. The response was always the same, "And just who do you think is going to say anything to her? I am not ready to end my career over her exposure desires." So, the topic was never discussed with Doris and she continued to be the hottest topic for office gossip and most avoided person in the company.

Nola-Jean Sugar and Doris Honey could be best friends. Let's meet Nola-Jean. She is a petite southern woman who grew up an only child. She became a best friend with several items of interest as a teenage girl. The list is as follows: blue eye shadow, an eye lash curler, big hair, very blonde with a touch of black root, blush (and lots of it), blouses that were approximately two sizes too small for her ample bust and let's not forget her favorite, skin tight pants. Nola-Jean's favorite comment in the office is "I wouldn't be seen without lipstick, it's just not professional". Like Doris Honey, Nola-Jean can attribute her management title to spending quality time with the boss.

Nola-Jean is a busy lady and she let's you know about it daily. Afterall, it takes a huge amount of time and energy to look the way she does and stay in the good graces of her male boss. "I'm just swamped!" was Nola-Jean's response to any question by a co-worker. This of course is a common response in the Deep South from a lady of her character.

This woman was no stranger to inappropriate office conversation. Nola-Jean just loved to talk about SEX. Most of the office was mindful of the intimate schedule she shared with her husband. She was always delighted to discuss the various strategic uses for whipped cream with any staff member!

Chapter 17
Sixteen & Seventeen - SEX! SEX! SEX! SEX! SEX! SEX! SEX!

Raging Hormones! This phenomenon defines where the focus is in this stage of the adolescent's development. One can only imagine what would be found in the brains of these adolescents if a medical test were to be developed that could read thought processes. Most parents shudder to even think of the test results on their teenager. I believe this must be when the phrase "tunnel vision" came onto the scene. These teenagers seem to be incapable of thinking of anything else, to the detriment at times of their school grades, parent and family cohesiveness or future college goals. It is a time when many parents begin to question the reasons they desired children in the first place. Somewhere close to eighteen years of age and high school graduation, the teenager begins to show some semblance of maturity and forward thinking. Sex is no longer the number one topic of their consciousness as well as unconsciousness. Parents begin to cautiously breathe easier and again feel thankful for being blessed with having the little precious child.

Unfortunately, for the rest of the world, some of these predominately sex focused adolescents never grow out of this stage. Corporate America does not escape having their fare share of these stunted adolescent minded adults in the business arena.

Carrie Hootchee was a stunning woman. She was tall, lean, and wore the perfect makeup combination to hide the flaws and accentuate the positives. Her dress was always of the latest trend and she carried herself straight and tall, projecting an aura of total self-confidence and admiration of herself. Carrie did not seem to mind or even acknowledge that the majority of the employees did not have this same admiration for her, either personally or professionally. Carrie had reached her mid-level management position on her terms without the support of others. She was not a team player in any sense of the word except in the one on one playing with the opposite sex outside of the office hours. Of course, her team player had to be in a position to further her career growth in the company. One admirable attribute that Carrie did have was loyalty. As long as this person was in a position and willing to assist her, she would remain totally devoted to him and only him.

A highly valued employee trait for employees to have in the constant evolving business environment of today is the ability to accept and move with change and Carrie was very adept to surviving in this dynamic environment. One relationship Carrie had endured for over five years with a senior level executive, Craig. Her title and position was elevated with each passing year. That is until Craig decided to take a wife and immediately start a family. However, being the ever-surviving artist that she was, this did not present a problem for her. Carrie quickly changed directions and began to focus on building a close relationship with another senior executive.

Erick Panus was the manager in charge of the administration department for a mid-sized company. Erick's sexual appetite for the females in his department was all but mid-sized. It was ravenous and well known throughout the company at all levels. However, since he was able to get great production from his department, upper management turned their heads and pretended not to acknowledge Erick's blatant illegal behavior. Erick had no qualms about letting his latest prey know that to not oblige his desires could seriously jeopardize their career with the company.

In sales driven companies, the administrative positions are there to support the sales force and in most cases represent the lower pay range in the company. The clerks working in these positions do not feel as empowered as the employees in the upper pay ranges and are more reluctant to take the matter to Human Resources or another manager for fear of losing their employment. The Ericks of the world feed on this fear and intimidation.

Erick's behavior became bolder as time went by until finally he was actually caught by another department manager in the storage room having sex with a clerk. The department manager immediately took the matter to upper level management. Realizing their potential legal liability, senior management could no longer stick their head in the sand for the sake of higher productivity and Erick was promptly terminated.

Erick Panus did not have the luck of Sabrina Irish. Sabrina could be described as the female equivalent to Erick with a twist! Sabrina was a Vice President of Communications for a mid-sized company. She was a striking six-foot red head weighing one hundred and twenty pounds soaking wet. Sabrina wore only designer suits with stiletto heels and her hair was always in the latest fashion upsweep. The male counterparts in the office guarded their positions carefully as she was shifty, unkind and a "devil" at business.

The office gossip was that if Sabrina wanted you out of the organization, it was only a matter of weeks before a member of senior management promptly dismissed you. Why? What did Sabrina say or do that generated such a quarry in the office? How did she have so much power over the actions of others?

Sabrina had special apparatus that she sharpened to secure her position and remain the only female Vice President in the company. Sabrina, being a single and beautiful woman used her charm against what she considered the weaker sex, MEN.

The men in the company that Sabrina handled with her allure were endless. The list is rumored as follows: three Board members, the CEO and three departmental managers. It was a mystery to most as to how she was able to sustain SEVEN MEN without one sexual harassment filing against her actions. What was Sabrina's secret to such scandal and sex in the workplace? The answer; she only carried on her affairs with married men. All of these lovers were prominent, six figure plus men that supported families with wives who would have half of their earnings in alimony and the other half in child support if she decided to tell their secret. The ultimate secret; Sabrina was the best of friends with each lover's wife. She insisted upon spending time with her friends and learned every intimate detail of the marriages. She took her lover's children to movies and watched them at sporting events. "Aunt Sabrina" gave the best gifts to the children! Sabrina had all of them in a bizarre position and she used it to secure her position at work and eliminate anyone that she felt or believed was a threat to her continued success.

SEX allowed Sabrina to communicate from between the sheets and beyond!

Corporate America's Misbehaving Children

Chapter 18
Eighteen And In Charge Of My Own Destiny

The teenage years are a continuing challenge for parents to survive without turning completely gray or going bald. When we hear parents of sixteen and seventeen year olds complain about their struggles with their teenagers, memories of our children's later adolescent years flood our minds and the only thing we can tell them is to hang on because the best challenges are yet to come. There is not a match for the adolescent when he or she turns the BIG EIGHTEEN! This adolescent time period is like a roller coaster ride. You feel relief and great joy when they do something that actually reflects well on your many years of training, modeling and rewarding good behaviors. Just when you begin to relax and feel good about your parenting skills, this "legally adult" teenager will do something that will cause you to question whether or not you were even there during his maturation growth. The clinical term Multiple Personality comes to mind.

Pat Scatterfield was just such a dual faceted person. Some days his conduct and mannerisms were of the most mature professionalism of any executive directing and overseeing a large company. Other days the employees would wonder just who was in Pat's big office sitting in the big chair behind the big desk. On these days, Pat's behavior would give a mental image of a small child sitting in the big chair throwing a big temper tantrum.

When Pat's staff entered the office each morning, they would first put their lunches or other items in their work area and then venture towards Pat's office to test the waters to see which personality Pat was harboring that day. Depending on which personification he was donning for the day determined how many cups of coffee they needed to down before their first encounter with him. If Pat's dark side emerged, the staff would gather quickly so they could plan the many tactics and maneuvers needed to make themselves unavailable for any meetings or discussions with him that day. Their workload would suddenly be tremendous and all time consuming.

Pat's dark side would rant and rave, stomp around the office like a herd of elephants so all would hear and be aware of his impending presence. Pat would criticize employees openly and in front of others until they just wanted to find a desk to crawl under and stay until the end of the day. No one was safe from this sinister persona.

On Pat's good days he was the model of an intelligent, focused, results driven, strategic team player and leader. He would hold staff meetings and seek input from everyone present, complimenting all suggestions made by his staff. During these times, Pat could make everyone in the room feel important and necessary for the department's success. These were the great times. Unfortunately, Mr. Goodness was never a long time resident.

Flagellation is a very important sport among teenage boys that parents continually work to discourage. Hopefully, by the time these boys are old enough to leave home for higher education or the business world they have outgrown this childish boyhood exercise in phewtility. Parents work very hard for over eighteen years to be able to launch an intelligent, groomed, and well-mannered adult onto the world.

Mitchell Winder was never able to progress from this adolescent stage. Mitchell was the President of a subsidiary of a very large organization. He was extremely intelligent about the business product, results oriented, bottom-line focused and a team player. Mitchell was always receptive to input from his

Corporate America's Misbehaving Children

employees at all levels on major decisions, even if it conflicted with his. If not for his one retained boyish trait of uncontrolled flagellation, he could have been a contestant for Time Magazine's Executive of the Year.

When the new Human Resources Manager, Victoria, was hired into Mitchell's company, it was not long until all of the other department managers were in Victoria's office complaining about Mitchell's unflattering personal trait of flagellating as he walked through the office and even during meetings. Victoria was appalled that someone at his level would act in such a primitive manner and was reluctant to believe what she was hearing. When the department managers insisted that Victoria counsel Mitchell on this subject, she naturally refused. Victoria did not feel she had not been with the organization long enough to tackle a counseling of this magnitude. She was not ready to allow his arrested development result in her unemployment so quickly.

A year goes by and Victoria finds herself sitting in on a counseling session with Mitchell and the Marketing Director, James. Mitchell and James were constantly at odds on what the Marketing Department's focus should be. Mitchell became increasingly dissatisfied with James's performance and scheduled a meeting with him to discuss his performance and what Mitchell's expectations were going forward. As with any formal counseling session, Victoria, the Human Resources Manager was asked to sit in as a witness and facilitator.

As Mitchell discussed at length the areas where he was dissatisfied with James's performance, it became very apparent to Victoria that James was becoming more and more agitated and was literally waiting in anticipation for Mitchell to pause so he could make his jump. When the opportunity arose, James went into a long dissertation about how Mitchell was the topic of gossip and laughter among the employees because of his constant flagellation as he walked though the office and in meetings. James shared with Mitchell that he and other managers were reluctant to include him in meetings with their clients because this disgusting behavior caused them immeasurable embarrassment. At this point in the discussion, James promptly got up, exited the room and left Victoria alone with Mitchell.

Victoria was stunned. It was now just her and Mitchell left in the room and the silence was deafening. After what seemed to be an eternal pause, Mitchell looked at Victoria and ask her if what James said about the employees gossiping was true. Victoria replied that yes, it was and suggested that Mitchell might want to see a doctor about the condition. Mitchell appeared to be graciously thankful for Victoria's advise.

To Victoria, it was totally incomprehensible that a person of James's position could have behaved in the manner he did at the meeting and even more mystifying to her was how Mitchell could have missed the basic child rearing fundamentals of manners and appropriate behavior. How Mitchell rose to the elevated position he held was a mystery to all.

Chapter 19
It All Happened So Fast!

The eighteen to twenty-one years of rearing a child to adulthood is quite a responsibility for a parent. The moment that tiny baby is handed to you until he or she is considered an adult seems like a lifetime to some of us. The first five years are filled with such wonder and milestones that you find it difficult to remember your life without children. The sleepless nights are forgotten as your child masters a new task. The joy is overwhelming as a parent nurtures them from one step to the next. It is a gift to watch life through their eyes. The years of elementary school are exciting as you learn again with your children. The years of secondary education bring you back to the days of being a teenager and wondering how this experience will turn out. It is awesome to watch your child develop into a thinking, feeling and mature adult. It is also a time of panic and anxiety for a parent because they are aware of the problems and dangers that exist outside of the secure home created for the child. Your child of course is aware that crime and punishment exist; yet because of their belief in their own mortality think that it will never happen to them. It is the longest yet shortest journey a parent will ever take in this life.

The same can be said for an employee choosing a career and watching it develop, grow and nurture. The employee begins the journey of building a career with very high hopes and expectations. The corporate ladder is to be climbed as high as possible for some while others are happy to simply be employed, pay their bills, support the family and have some money left over for the non-essentials of life. The early years of working are exciting, as you are self-sufficient and truly an adult since you are out in the world earning a living. The years that follow are about continued economic responsibility and personal achievement for many individuals. It is the desire to do better financially, learn more and stay active in society by making a working contribution. It is also about dissolution for those who jump into the business area with idealistic thoughts.

For those of us who have worked in Human Resources, it is a gift to watch employees strive for excellence and truly put their heart and soul into a job. There is no greater feeling than to offer someone a job opportunity on behalf of an employer and watch that employee soar with positive performance appraisals and promotions. There is also no worse feeling than seeing an employee fail in a position despite all odds and being fired. The most difficult job of all for a Human Resource Professional is working through a reduction in force with an employee. It is a situation that is never quite understood by either party no matter how much it is explained by the leaders of an organization. It is especially difficult for the Human Resource Professional as they are often the executors of this fate or the person charged to assist a department manager or supervisor with the action. It is irrelevant as to whether you agree or disagree with the decision. It is your professional obligation to act in good faith for your employer.

In today's business environment, there are very few individuals that have not been personally affected by downsizing, layoff, reduction in force, restructuring or whatever the latest trendy term may be. As a result, we have a workforce of eager yet suspicious employees. The day of the gold watch for retirement is few and far between. A disciplined employee can only continue to put one foot in front of the other as a toddler does in great faith and take the job, one day at a time. It is with great discipline, hard work, faith in a higher being than one's self and a desire to continue to do what you enjoy for a living that keeps you pursuing your chosen career. In many cases the time from eager beginnings to dissolution in our careers is much shorter than the twenty-one years spent preparing for the adult work world.

When Susie Wunder graduated from College with a business degree in Organizational Behavior and Management, she felt confident that she now had the skills and knowledge needed for the corporate business world that would ensure her future for herself and her family. Susie was a dedicated and hard worker no matter what the task she was responsible for. Many had referred to her as having more tenacity than anyone they had ever met. Susie's tenacity was a direct product of her childhood. She came from a broken home caused by a parent's alcohol addiction. There was never much money in the home for anything outside of survival items so Susie always had dreams of what she would do as an adult to make her life better. Going to college was the most important goal for Susie because she saw it as the only way to rise above her humble beginnings. Of course her family was not able to pay for college attendance forcing Susie to put this dream goal on hold for sometime. Never forgetting what she had always seen as her way out of the situation of her childhood, she remained steadfastly focused on her college degree goal for over nineteen years while raising her own family. When Susie's youngest child entered Kindergarten, she enrolled in the local university. At the time Susie was working a full time forty-hour week job and with her husband raising three children ages fourteen, thirteen, and five.

Susie was determined to finish the four-year degree plan in five years even though she was going part-time. She accomplished this goal by taking courses year round, denying herself the luxury of any summer breaks. This rigorous schedule allowed Susie to accomplish her goal and graduate in five years according to her original plan.

When Susie got her first job in her career field for a well-respected company, she excitedly marched into her new office with framed diploma in hand ready to hang on the wall for all to see. This diploma validated who she was and why she was offered the position. Susie was eager to get started so she could demonstrate what a great team player she could be, her strong analytical skills, strategic thought processes and people management skills. Susie's long dreamt about career was in her grasp now and getting off the ground. She was very excited and ready to jump in and try and make a difference in the organization. Susie was impressed with the other employees' work ethics, skill levels, experiences and team player attitudes.

Most of Susie's family members and relatives had worked for one or maybe two companies through out their careers. This long employee tenure fostered a family type environment for everyone. This was the kind of environment Susie expected to work in and it did begin in that way because her first company was a young company in business less than five years and only had forty-seven employees of which at least twelve traveled most of the time.

As the company began to grow and employee count increased, the family feeling became weaker and weaker. With the strong growth, Senior Management needed to bring in more mid-level managers and supervisors to oversee the day-to-day operations of each department. For the most part, these managers were brought in from outside of the company. It was not long until the employees began to notice a lot of changes in the company, initiated by the "new kids on the block". The family style culture became less and less and the previous team culture was being replaced with the "everything is done to increase the bottom-line" philosophy. This was when Susie first began to feel the dissolution of her life long goal.

After twenty years of being disillusioned in Corporate America's everything for the bottom-line philosophy no matter what the cost to integrity, honesty, moral values and least of all the employees, Susie finally called it quits for good the last time she was laid off. The one lesson Susie did learn was that having and openly demonstrating the values of integrity, honesty, open communication, empathy and strong morals that were valued in her upbringing would most likely result in eventual unemployment in the adult world. Many times these values are in direct conflict to the bottom-line mentality held by some senior executives. The disillusionment became too difficult to deal with on a daily basis.

Many companies do not understand the cost to their bottom line in hidden dollars when they lose the dedicated, talented and motivated employees like Susie. The day of enlightening will come however when there are no more Susie's in the workplace.

Corporate America's Misbehaving Children

Chapter 20
The Body Count

In war times, the body count of enemies, allies, and our own troops are watched and counted diligently. Sometimes the mission given to soldiers by a Commander is a simple one - increase the enemy body count. This can come from the Commander in Chief in the White House, a field Commander or any Commander down the chain of command. It is very important for news correspondents to have the correct balance of casualties to report. In all wars, the enemy must sustain a higher body count in order for the military to continue to have the government's and public citizen's support. The wider the void between our numbers and the enemies' numbers in our favor, the stronger the support from the American public, which must be sustained for the military and government leaders to continue on their path to victory.

Corporate America is also a war zone with many casualties. In this war zone there can be more than one Demilitarized Zone (DMZ) line, a buffer zone between the good guys and the bad guys. The front line is usually located between the line managers and the mid-level managers. The advance line is between the mid-level and executive levels and the victory line is drawn between each executive vying to capture and overthrow the top position of the commanding officer, CEO/President.

The corporate warlords aspiring to conquer the next level in the organization sees himself or herself as the good guy and all others that stand between them and victory as the bad guys. These perceived bad guys could be peer managers, senior managers and even the employees in lower positions. The corporate warlords plan their covert strategy in detail on how they should cross the DMZ undetected to search and destroy any enemy in the way of their conquest. In many cases, by the time the warlord manager's intent is recognized, it is too late. Bodies are strewn everywhere with some thrown out of the war zone completely and into the unemployment zone.

Pat Whippy was a mid-level warlord manager seeking to advance herself forward at all cost. She went through her staff at the speed of light. The body count in Pat's department was always high. Pat was bent on becoming a key executive who would be given recognition, authority and rewards at all cost. Technically, Pat was excellent at what she did but her ability to communicate with others or provide leadership to her staff was incredibly deficient. Pat was totally devoid of compassion, compromise, facilitation or any of the many people skills needed to be a leader. But then, Pat was not interested in leading; she was pushing her way upward and leaving many bodies along the way.

Pat hounded her manager consistently about wanting the recognition she felt was deserved and she was eventually given a title of Vice President and a monetary reward (bonus). Her manager surrendered not because he agreed with her but because he could not take her constant nagging and whining any longer. Without realizing it, he had become one of her victims and added to her personal body count number.

Unfortunately for others, this surrender by her manager only increased her evaluation and admiration of herself and lack of respect for others. Pat began to scold her staff harder and over even more trivial items. Pat's revolving door for hiring and replacing members of her staff began to swing even faster with bodies flying at record speed. The hidden cost to the company in lost production was considerable, but so what, she was now a Vice President.

About The Author

The authors of Corporate America's Misbehaving Children have thirty plus years in the field of Human Resources and their motivation for writing this book of stories and analogies was the overwhelming similarities they observed between their experiences in watching their children grow up and move through the many maturation stages as they strive to reach adulthood and some of the behaviors of the adults observed at all levels in the corporate professional environment. Their desire is for the reader to be able to connect with their analogies and stories and laugh, relate and tell his or her own story about one or many of the characters or scenarios in the book.

Printed in the United Kingdom
by Lightning Source UK Ltd.
102908UKS00001B/334-342